How I
Published
4 Books in
6 Years

(mistakes included)

by

Russell S. Smith

OTHER BOOKS BY RUSSELL S. SMITH

Non-fiction

The Gun That Wasn't There

No Reason to Kill

One Policeman's Lights and Siren

Outdoor Memoirs

Steps into God's Country

Great effort was made to try to confirm each fact within the following pages; but unless otherwise noted, the author and publisher make no explicit guarantees as to the accuracy of the information contained in this work.

The cover was designed by Anne-Charlotte Patterson (Southern Combustion Creative, www.southerncombustion.com).

ISBN: 1484935322
ISBN-13: 9781484935323

Library of Congress Control Number: 2013909197
CreateSpace Independent Publishing Platform
North Charleston, South Carolina

ACKNOWLEDGMENT

My thanks go out to my mother, June Smith, and my sister, Becky Smith, for giving the manuscript a look over; and to Areta Robinson, Kathy Robinson and Linda Hermes – a special team of friends – and my wife Linda who proofread the drafts and offered editing suggestions that helped produce the final product. My special thanks go to author Skipper Duncan for his humbling comment on the back cover; and to Anne-Charlotte Patterson for her cover design.

DEDICATION

This work is dedicated to the memory of:

Award winning western writer

Elmer Kelton;

And

Noted historian, newspaperman and author

Ross McSwain.

TABLE OF CONTENTS

PREFACE

"I am going to write a book someday." I have heard those words from people many times since I published my first book **The Gun That Wasn't There**. Most times they were followed with, "How did you do it? How did you get it published?"

My writing life began when I entered Uvalde Junior High School about fifty years ago. I wrote rhyming sentences (which I called poems) and short stories in spiral notebooks. In high school, several of my poems were accepted for publication in national high school anthologies.

Two high school events have stayed with me all these years. My Uvalde High School senior English teacher, Mae H. Crump, gave me an A for content and a C for mechanics on my last research paper. She said, "You may never write the story right, but you sure have a way of telling it."

The second event took several of us into the high school library to meet with a college professor. "How many of you think you want to write for a living?" she asked. We all raised our hands. She quietly put a can of beans on the table and said, "Then you had better get used to eating these." I didn't realize at the time that I would spend more than 20 years writing police reports but either way she was right about the beans.

"You have to build your resume," my friend and author Joe Gibson told me in the fall of 1978. His words came after I had received many rejections from magazines that I'd sent articles to. "Give a few stories away; then you can say you've been published." I gave a story about the illicit drug phencyclidine (known as Angel Dust) to Reserve Law News. In 1980, I received my first paycheck from Police Product News for a similar story. The cover of the slick national magazine depicted an angel digging a grave. I joined the San Angelo Writers' Club during this time and learned many things from members and their guest speakers.

I received my first paycheck for writing about phencyclidine (street name Angel Dust) in Police Product News in 1980.

The Texas Municipal Police Association started producing their TMPA Quarterly magazine in the early 1980s. I wrote for them for years, a nonfiction article and a fiction mystery about every 90 days. It was also where I produced my first outdoor column which later led to my relationship with the San Angelo Standard-Times newspaper, Texas Fish and Game Magazine, Texas

Sportsman, Fishing and Hunting News, Ranch and Rural Living and others.

I wrote for magazines and newspapers for more than 25 years before publishing my first book.

In 1984, I published a book of poems entitled **One Policeman – A Different Perspective**. It was a short run of 59-pages (200 copies) that luckily for me sold out quickly. Twenty-three years later I published **The Gun That Wasn't There.** It was then that I started getting the questions, "How did you do it, how did you get it published?" The answer is provided inside the following pages of **How I Published 4 Books in 6 Years** (mistakes included).

INTRODUCTION

The book **How I Published 4 Books in 6 Years** is divided into three parts. Part one gives a few insights into how I came to write my books and a few processes that I used to write them. Part two is what this work is all about, providing a look into the process I used to self-publish my books. The final part details how I have marketed my works; and all parts include mistakes I've made along the way.

These are the things I did to make my dream "to write and publish books" come true. This is how I did it. Yet what works for me may not be what is best for everyone else, but this answers the question of how I did it.

PART ONE

THE STORY

I believe that every book begins with a story developed within the mind, supported by facts or by imagination. My first book began in 1989 when I met the former Terrell County Sheriff, Bill Cooksey, who was then the Director of Law Enforcement and Fire Training at Odessa College in Odessa, Texas. I was a Sergeant with the San Angelo, Texas Police Department and was at the college trying to recruit police applicants.

It was the first time I heard even a tiny piece of the history about a man who terrorized citizens during the 1960s in the Texas Hill Country and West Texas; a man who shot the Postmaster at Pumpville and later the Terrell County Sheriff. As I drove home that day, and a year later after I interviewed Cooksey and his wife, I knew I had the beginnings of a story worthy of publication; a story that needed to be told for historical reasons and to educate others about the gun that wasn't there, not realizing it would be the title when the book was completed.

Unfortunately, the book was not fully researched and published for more than seventeen years. While I would like to say that the challenges I faced in gathering all the facts led to this late timeline, I must confess my first mistake – that it was rather a character flaw that kept me saying, "I am going to publish a book someday," while the research materials sat on my shelves.

PROCRASTINATION

I have always been one of those people who have a lot of irons in the fire. Rather than deal with all of them on a current basis, I have been known to procrastinate until the last minute or much longer than I should have. The best definition that describes my condition comes from Dictionary.com, "The act or habit of procrastinating, or putting off or delaying, especially something requiring immediate attention." Hence, I used to be a person who said, "I am going to write a book someday," until two things happened to help me turn it around.

First, Pastor Paul Shero gave me a copy of the book **The First Five Pages** written by literary agent Noah Lukeman. The gist is that people make up their mind about a book within the first five pages. Yet, Lukeman wrote other words that helped me to go forward, including:

"Most of the truly great artists have broken all the rules – and this is precisely what has made them great," and, "The art of writing cannot be taught, but the craft of writing can."

The second thing was actually one of those "spam" emails that came into my computer on August, 5, 2004. I was busy deleting a group of them when I read the following in the subject line, "If you knew you were going to die tomorrow." On the page below I read something like – If you knew you were going to die tomorrow, what person or persons would you want to spend that time with, or what thing or things would you want to do? Then I deleted it.

I wish I would never have deleted that email. I didn't just delete it. I re-deleted them all out of the deleted file before I went on with my business. By the time I went to bed that night, the words "If you…" were spinning through my head – and they have been there since I first read them.

After that night, I started attaching "help me" sayings to the walls of my home office. The most appropriate for this chapter follows first, along with a few others.

"If we did all the things we were capable of, we
would literally astound ourselves."
Thomas Edison

"Dream as if you will live forever…
Live as if you only have today."
Author Unknown

"The desire to succeed is useless without the
willingness to prepare."
Author Unknown

And

"Success seems to be largely a matter of hanging
on after others have let go."
William Feather

GETTING IT DONE

It took a number of months, in the midst of a fulltime job, to travel several thousand miles, interview numerous people, buy and gather records, take photographs and then agonize for days in front of the computer screen before the first draft was completed. It was during that research time that I found the title that made its way onto the cover of the published book.

My family members were enjoying a few wonderful days of R&R at the Dry Hollow Hideaway near Paint Rock when I delivered an overview of the story I had in my mind. My aunt Daisy Diaz-Alemany, PhD, LPC, raised her hand and she said, **"The Gun That Wasn't There,"** and we had our title.

The editing process then and now begins by emailing the draft to my friend Linda Hermes. She looks at the project two ways – first as a comprehension issue, letting me know whether a lay person might understand what I was trying to say. Her response might be, "What are you trying to say here? Or, "I don't understand this." She also checks for grammar and spelling, as does my friend Areta

Robinson who is given a hardcopy of the manuscript. Her paper copy always comes back with plenty of red marks throughout. Her daughter Kathy helps too and her suggestions may come back in a different color of ink.

I do not print the hardcopy at home. The cost of ink is just too high. I take the manuscript (on a USB drive) to a store that does such printing. It is a lot more affordable, especially since I may have copies of as many as three drafts printed before publication.

After the manuscript is looked over several times, copies are given to my mother, my sister and my wife so they can look for misspelled words. I have learned that those who have already read it several times may miss misspelled words on a third or fourth reading. Such words may jump out to a new reader. Separate hardcopies of the manuscript are given to the readers after they are hole-punched and entered into three-ring binders.

Draft copies of **<u>Steps into God's Country</u>** *ready for the proof-readers.*

Maude's Family

…and Thomas B. Clubb was one of the early settlers at Montell. Born in South …1848, the ship captain married Louisiana native Maria(h) Carr in Jefferson County. …44. The couple lived on Mustang Island, just across the bay from Corpus Christi, …y members operated light houses. The wife feared for his life on the sea so at her *her husband's* …er a hurricane destroyed everything they had, they settled along Montell Creek in …unty when they moved to Montell around 1875.¹ By 1882, Captain Clubb was Justice …e, at times assisting Sheriff H.W. Baylor with judicial duties."

… interesting point in family history, according to a Cameron County deed dated …, 1957, involved land owned by Thomas B. Clubb. A contract drawn up in 1947 …given family members 1/16th interest in all mineral rights for land described as, …of what is known as Padre Island… either in or at the eastern edge of the counties of …illacy, Kennedy, Kleberg and Nueces… and any of said counties bordering the Gulf …(But apparently no valuable consideration ever came from said contract because my …s didn't own a car and walked to town to order their groceries the whole time I knew

…ly records also include notice of a suit involving the site of large oil discoveries near …A story in the Dallas Morning News began with, "Thousands Try to Claim Pelham …eague. Clubb's daughter Agnes Maria had married a man named Parry Humphreys, … kin to those who held rights to those lands."

…n-law John McGowan, who *was* married to Clubb's daughter Sarah, also moved his …ntell. They built a cedar log house along Cedar Creek. The couple had six

Corrected hardcopy comes back with notes and email responses in different colors of ink.

Once I thought the manuscript was ready, I gave a copy to Ross McSwain, a newspaperman and historian who already had a number of books under his belt. The look on his face told the whole story when I returned to talk to him about it. "Where did all those commas come from? I've never seen so many commas," said Ross, who continued, "Tell the story! It's a true story – take all the other crap out."

I am a visually oriented person and yes I had embellished part of the book, especially the part about the Bandit and his relationship with a beautiful prostitute in Mexico. I spent a month removing about 10,000 words and a lot of commas. Then I took McSwain and Elmer Kelton what I hoped was the final draft. A few days later, McSwain said, "That's more like it."

Elmer Kelton told me he didn't know if he would have time to read the draft when I took it to him that Thursday. He was busy writing two books of his own, but on the following Monday, he called and asked me to come by. He handed me an introduction that he had written and told me, "It has everything they want in the movies."

THE PUBLISHER

Cactus Book Shop owner Felton Cochran initially suggested that I send **The Gun That Wasn't There** to a Houston publisher who had a good West Texas distribution market. I sent the following items to the editor/publisher in February 2006: 300-page double spaced copy of the manuscript including endnotes, copy of the photographs, copy of the photograph bibliography, my resume and three CDs. One CD included a copy of the Microsoft Word written manuscript with endnotes. The second and third included a large group of photographs, many more than were included in the final book. Self-addressed stamped envelopes were also included.

I talked with the editor/publisher several times. He told me the book held promise. I was excited but I never did receive a contract. My daddy died and I was deeply disappointed he didn't get to see the book in print. Then a rumor surfaced that the publisher had things on hold while he dealt with a financial situation I'd not known about. Shortly thereafter, in November 2006, I sent him a letter stating the following, "I appreciate your consideration of my book project, **The Gun That**

Wasn't There, but I have decided to publish the book now. My dad died this summer, my mom is in her mid-70s and I want her to see it in print." I requested he send my manuscript back to me. (I did not use names here because the editor/publisher has since passed away and the company closed.)

The bottom line was that I was going to take total control of my project. I was going to become not only an author but also the publisher and distributor of my work.

PART TWO

FINDING A PRINTER

My search to find a publishing company to print my books took about a month. I talked with Ross McSwain who along with Harold Byler had just published **Texas Politics and Greed** through a company called AuthorHouse Publishing. I contacted them and several others through the Internet and had their materials sent to me. I talked with Felton Cochran and the manager of the local Hastings Books, Music and Entertainment store. I bought a number of self-published books and looked at their cover design along with text and photograph clarity. Then Tom Green County Justice of the Peace Eddie Howard suggested that I talk with local author Carol Smith who had authored **Journey to Command** about the Top Gun flight school. This final advice would ultimately lead me to the company I've been using ever since.

Ms. Smith told me to call a woman named Lynn who worked for an Amazon owned company named BookSurge. (BookSurge and a sister company named CreateSpace soon merged and hereafter in this book will be called CreateSpace.)

I called CreateSpace Publishing Consultant Lynn Eang Yib (1-843-225-5458) at her office in South Carolina. She told me they had an online site, www.createspace. com, that allows a person to publish a manuscript, or I could use their professional services and have my book published. I am not a very tech savvy person so I told her I preferred to send them my manuscript and photographs and have them format and publish my book. I emailed her (leang@createspace.com) a few questions before I finally made my decision to use their company.

I bought their Author Advantage Program for $499 which allowed my Word document manuscript to be converted into a professionally formatted Adobe PDF design. The package allowed the use of ten photographs and I paid to use a few more. I also paid $199 for a hardcover upgrade that produced a beautiful jacketed hardback copy of **The Gun That Wasn't There**. I did not use their cover design and will discuss this in another chapter.

(I have bought a CreateSpace publishing package for each book. I have noticed that costs have come down quite a bit since I published my first book. My last package called the Total Design Freedom Custom Package was $379. These packages include the Word document conversion to PDF, the index and endnotes, adding my name and the name of the book to recurring pages and formatting the words into a book design format. The Kindle pricing used to be $199 and now it is at $69 for a secure encrypted version.)

CREATESPACE

I should say up front that I was pretty confused when I first called Lynn about getting my book published. I'm the guy who gets a cell phone and continually goes back where I got it so they can show me how to use it. However I did find their website and established my account. (Yes, I wrote the password down so I would be able to get back in later.)

Signing in to the website, I was guided to my own Member Dashboard page where the name of my book(s) appeared. There was a unique ID number for my account. The page guided me through the process of sending my manuscript and photographs for publication; and allowed me to order copies of my book at a rate much reduced from retail; and, it gives me a monthly report of books sold (through Amazon and CreateSpace).

The personalized account has a message center whereby CreateSpace can deliver information to you on an as needed basis and provides you with a Contact Support icon to give you guidance for questions about publishing, ordering, payment/royalties, distribution or other options. As this is written, my Dashboard has the words "Attention Required" in red letters beside the title **How I Published 4 Books in 6 Years** letting me know that my next step is to download the manuscript and photographs.

Today, their webpage also guides you to free online tools and a place to upload your files for free. I believe this is for people who already have their manuscript and pages laid out in PDF "ready to print" format. They do this for authors, musicians and filmmakers, and they have a new Custom Cover Design Services Section.

SENDING THE MANUSCRIPT AND PHOTOGRAPHS

I chose a 6- by 9-inch size for each of my books (authors are allowed to choose from 15 different sizes). My Microsoft Word typed-manuscript headings were written in Times New Roman 14-point type and the basic manuscript in 12-point. I inserted page breaks at the start of each new chapter. Then I went to the CreateSpace website and downloaded my manuscript and photographs via the Internet.

I had previously filled out a few forms telling them about the book, my biography (simple) and I finally talked with their development people and used 12-point type for **The Gun That Wasn't There.** Each of my following books has been published in the larger 14-point type so it is easier to read.

My photographs were sent at 300 dpi and in the size I wanted them to appear in the book. As an example, since the pages are 6- by 9-inches, most of my photographs were 4- by 6-inches or less. A question I've heard a lot is, "How do you know where to put your photographs?" Their guidelines tell you to place < before and after the words insert image and the following file number or name. The caption is listed below it in the manuscript.

(12 pt)

INTRODUCTION

Texas folklore offers many stories of phantoms, most of which raised questions never answered and left mysteries unsolved. Examples are the legends of the wild woman of the Navidad River, the "murder steer" of the Davis Mountains, and la llorona, the wraith-like mother roaming the banks of Texas and Mexican rivers, crying for her drowned children.

INTRODUCTION

(14 pt)

Cops generally don't make good storytellers, but former Police Chief Russell Smith of San Angelo, Texas is an exception. His experiences as a police officer, police chief and as an award winning outdoor writer-photographer for a daily newspaper, as well as nationally recognized hunting and fishing publications, has helped provide him with another career. Readers of this unusual story about a brutal robbery-murder will be watching for more books to come.

This is an illustration of 12- point versus 14-point font size from Russell Smith's 2nd book **No Reason to Kill.**

What happens if you have questions during this process? You are assigned to a development team that you can contact by phone or email.

COVER DESIGN

Each of my book covers has been produced by graphic designer Anne-Charlotte Patterson from Austin, Texas. She is quite talented and has given me any number of examples from which to choose. She is the daughter-in-law of Bill Cooksey whom I wrote about in **The Gun That Wasn't There**. She offered a few thoughts about what helps her develop a suitable cover.

"Russell did an excellent job in describing his books (what the book is about). He provided photos and was clear about the schedule, budget and who/where the books were to be printed. (Then) He shared his cover design option with others, got feedback and then made a decision about which design to use."

I have sent Ms. Patterson a copy of all photographs I plan to use in the book, and most times all I have considered using but did not. CreateSpace provides a cover template to authors who have their covers designed elsewhere. I sent this via email to Ms. Patterson and she has used it for each book. I gave her a $500 budget for **The Gun That Wasn't There**, more or less for others.

Within a few weeks, she sent back 5 designs (8 for **No Reason to Kill**) for me to consider.

I don't have the means to hire a marketing firm to define what might be more attractive to potential readers. So with each cover selection, I have placed copies of each design in several three-ring binders and let people (of all ages) vote on which one they liked best. With **The Gun That Wasn't There**, a cover design displaying an empty gun holster was chosen the most.

Ms. Patterson called a few days after I gave her the vote results. She asked if I could find a holster and gun-belt to photograph with the cartridges in it. She asked that I lay the holster out on white poster board and photograph it several different ways: belt wrapped around holster and laid out flat, front and back. I didn't understand why until after I saw the final product. She explained that the spine might be the only thing showing on the shelf.

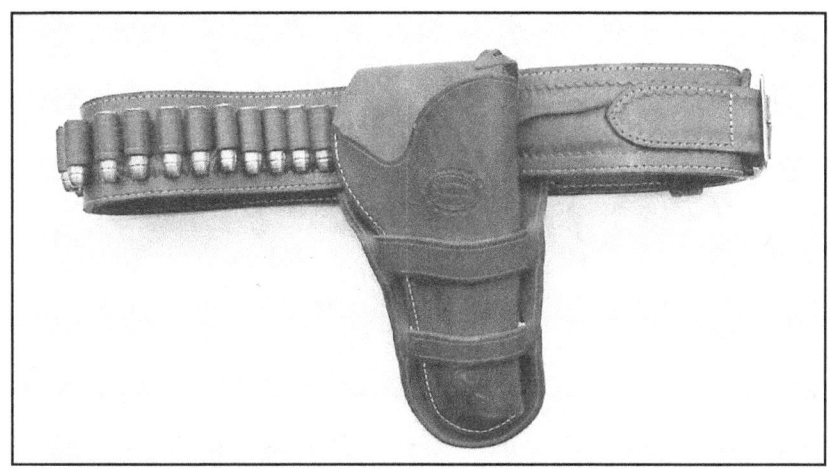

Anne-Charlotte Patterson asked Russell Smith to lay a holster and gun-belt out on white poster board and photograph it several ways.

*The final cover design for **The Gun That Wasn't There.***

Anne-Charlotte Patterson designed the spine so it would draw the reader's eye.

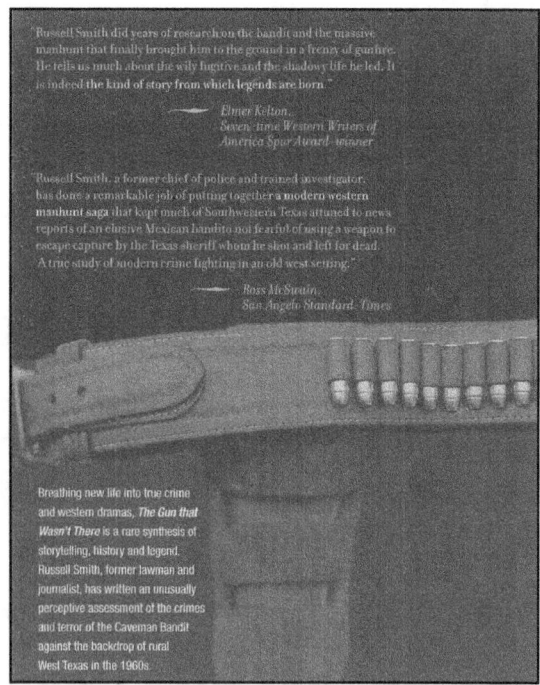

The back cover layout contains blurbs from Elmer Kelton and Ross McSwain.

Anne-Charlotte Patterson, art director for Southern Combustion Creative, may be contacted at southerncombustion@gmail.com, (512) 797-5034 or www.southerncombustion.com.

CreateSpace does have talented cover people too. I had them develop a cover for my second book **No Reason to Kill.** This blue and beige cover is shown on the back cover of **How I published 4 Books in 6 Years**. Their cover was shown to possible readers with the 8 others that Ms. Patterson provided me. The black cover with red letters shown on the front of this book received the greatest number of votes overall.

I should mention that the cover cannot be downloaded to CreateSpace until your manuscript has been arranged into a book format. The reason is because your cover designer must know the exact number of pages that are going to be in the book before they finalize the spine width. Once CreateSpace gave me the final page count, I was able to upload my cover to the company.

Note: While I let people of all ages vote on each book's cover designs, I have found that bookstore owners and managers might have a differing opinion. With **One Policeman's Lights and Siren**, I let these professionals override my vote and the vote of the masses. Each said, "You don't want two books with basically the same color."

A black cover was the most popular but the book came out with a red cover...

AN "ALMOST" MISTAKE

I was really getting excited by December 2006. My manuscript and cover were both at CreateSpace and I knew I would soon see the first copy of my book. Then my childhood memory banks recollected a deer hunter who was shot by a man who was burglarizing his hunting camp west of Uvalde (where I grew up). I just knew the culprit from **The Gun That Wasn't There** had done it (not the butler) and it would make a great additional chapter.

Here's the gist of the event –

Three men in a Jeep drive up to their cabin just after dark. A padlock is gone; the door open. One man grabs his deer rifle as he says, "I'll take care of this," and approaches the building. Three shots ring out from inside the building and the hunter falls to the ground. A slight built man runs out and away into the security of the darkness. The event happened within half a mile of the railroad tracks. The modus operandi, or the way the man committed the crime, did fit with the Bandit who terrorized parts of Uvalde County and West Texas during the 1960s.

The next morning I was in Brackettville, Texas studying the Kinney County death records. After hours of scouring the documents and not finding what I was looking for, a clerk said, "The records are probably in Uvalde, Del Rio or San Antonio, especially if they took him to a hospital there. I returned home empty handed late that Friday afternoon.

"I'm going to put a hold on my book because I think the Bandit might have killed a deer hunter in Kinney County. I gotta find the death record so I can see if bullets were recovered that could be matched to his gun. We could solve a murder," I told my friend Ross McSwain later that night.

McSwain was direct, "You already have a book. You publish it. You can always write a sequel if you locate what you are looking for."

Writing nonfiction history could lead anyone down another road here or there as they research their topic. Part of getting it done is to know when to stop and put it together. McSwain's words kept me from making a terrible mistake. Of course, I did not put the book on hold.

(Though I spent many days and plenty of hours later searching, I was never able to find a key piece of evidence that could have proven the Bandit committed the Kinney County crime.)

MORE MISTAKES

CreateSpace allows you a large number of corrections (if needed) when you get your manuscript proof copy. They list this in their contract materials but I never dreamed I would find so many as I went over my first formatted copy of **The Gun That Wasn't There**. In book form, other mistakes just jumped out at me and those who read the manuscript for me. The corrections were easy to make via the Internet and the CreateSpace software.

Today, I smile when I find a misspelled or misused word in a book written by a noted author. I am reminded of Noah Lukeman's words from his book **The First Five Pages**, "Even the most proficient writers cannot catch all of their own mistakes. Outside readers can see things you cannot."

NATURAL FRUSTRATION

I must confess, and would be remiss if I didn't, that I did have periods of natural frustration with the process of getting my books printed. Merriam-Webster probably defines this best as "a deep chronic sense or state of insecurity and dissatisfaction arising from unresolved problems or unfulfilled needs." I describe a few instances below.

Learning to use the CreateSpace software was a real challenge for me, though today I just breeze through it. The fact that I was not shy about asking for help from their support personnel helped get me through this, though, as I have said before, I am not a technically proficient person and it took a little getting used to with **The Gun That Wasn't There**.

No Reason to Kill educated me about timing in the book business. I started the book process during the summer and was ready to make my order shortly before Christmas, believing full well that I had given the company enough time to get my 3000 books to me. But I didn't realize it was like trying to put a large square dowel in a small round hole.

CreateSpace has timelines that may indicate they will have your books printed and to you by a certain date. The books come sooner, most of the time, as they did with **The Gun That Wasn't There**. However Christmas is a high demand time for books; Amazon and CreateSpace have tremendous workloads. I was frustrated and disappointed - but looking back now, at the big picture, I understand what they are dealing with.

Another frustration is just time. You have finished your work and you want it now. Your insides are revving up every minute that you don't have a copy of your book in your hands. You spent months and/or years writing it, you want it NOW. What is taking so long? With the first few books I did not understand why they couldn't just click a few buttons and get my book on to the next step in the process. Yet, today I understand they have a process that keeps things from going awry, and they are helping many people (at the same time) publish their book of a lifetime. Mistakes happen and they have a system to keep them to a minimum.

A final publishing frustration is that only softbacks are sold via the Internet through Amazon and CreateSpace. I have to buy the hardbacks and sell them myself. Contrary to the softback price, these finer works are more costly.

THE FINAL PROOF

I received the final proof copy of **<u>The Gun That Wasn't</u> <u>There</u>** in early February 2007. It was amazing to see my work in print. I read it from cover to cover, scanning every word and picture caption for any mistakes, though I found none. That night, I let my proofreaders give it a once over and each gave me a thumbs up.

The word **Proof** *is stamped inside the back cover of your proof copy.*

The next day, with the simple click of an approval button, **The Gun That Wasn't There** was BUY ready. It wasn't long before it showed up on the Amazon website and only two weeks before 1000 softback copies were delivered to my front door. (It was several more weeks before I received the hardback books.)

The day the books arrived can only be described as one of the highlights of my life.

Russell Smith removes a copy of his book **The Gun That Wasn't There** *from the cases delivered to his house. His neighbor Areta Robinson snapped the photo.*

A FEW FINAL THOUGHTS ABOUT PRINTING COMPANIES

CreateSpace is the company I have chosen to publish my books. I chose them because of their connection to Amazon and because of the clarity of their pictures. Though I can start the book process totally online now, I will always call Lynn and buy the formatting package from her. I like to talk to a person and I know their system now. I don't like change. This is just my preference and yours might be something totally different.

(If I were younger or really computer and software literate, I would buy and learn an Adobe PDF software package that would allow me to convert my Word document, lay out my photos and captions, number the pages and include the index and endnotes into a book format. It would allow me to reduce my cost and provide CreateSpace with a ready to print file and cover. Then I would just buy the books from them.)

If you are going to self-publish, I would suggest that you do your own research and find a company that works for you. Take your time and do your homework before making a decision about your life's work. You might find that a local printer can meet your needs.

My friend Ross McSwain used a number of printers during his lifetime. His last books, **Wornout Memories** and **Out Yonder and Beyond**, and that of agricultural historian and newspaperman Jerry Lackey, author of **Homestead – Pioneers of Texas' Frontier**, were printed by Ballinger Printing & Graphics, 906 Hutchins Avenue, Ballinger, Texas 76821 (325) 365-8206.

PART THREE

BOOK DELIVERY – IN AND OUT

My first order (1000 copies) of **The Gun That Wasn't There** was delivered to my house by truck. I paid the shipping costs from South Carolina. I had previously addressed 50 cardboard mailers so free-copies (advertising) could be sent to newspapers, magazines and movie production companies. The day they arrived, my neighbor, Areta Robinson, helped me get them ready to take to the U.S. Post Office.

Area newspapers did a great job mentioning the book in print. Rick Smith and Ross McSwain wrote about it in the San Angelo Standard-Times and later Glenn Dromgoole mentioned it in his book reviews. Several regional magazines highlighted the book while the large city papers and the national magazines did not.

The day after delivery, my friend, Jake Young, and I started a two-day route that took us to bookstores, newspapers and businesses throughout part of the Texas Hill Country. The week after, my wife and I spent a week contacting similar businesses on a route from Leakey to Uvalde, to Del Rio, to Langtry-Dryden-Sanderson and on to Alpine. The following week, Jake Young and I covered an area from Odessa to Abilene to Brownwood.

<u>The Gun That Wasn't There</u> was in 55 stores after our three jaunts. I call our trips a jaunt because it was fun and I learned a lot about the book business along the way. My first booksignings were at the Cactus Book Shop in San Angelo and then in Eldorado and Sanderson.

Cactus Book Shop owner Felton Cochran had already educated me about the book business by the time the books arrived. Book stores expect a 40% discount off the retail price for carrying a book. The businesses all bought their copies at that discount, except for Hastings which only does consignment for local authors.

Today, my books are regularly sold in 10 stores and a few others during the Christmas holidays, along with sales from Amazon and Kindle.

THE BUSINESS OF BOOKS

I obtained a Texas sales tax number for my business from the Texas State Comptroller's Office before the books arrived. Emails, letters and phone calls led to personal inscriptions and books being mailed via the United States Post Office and UPS, whichever was the least costly. The media rate for books at the Post Office is a great discount over regular mail, though with large orders it paid to check all rates.

Sales tax must be paid for retail sales in the area where the sale is made. If I am in Del Rio, I make an entry on the ledger for the amount paid and put Del Rio out beside it. However, they are all listed on one final tax form. San Angelo is where I have made my greatest number of retail sales. When you wholesale your book (product) to a business, they pay the sales tax on the retail cost.

I bought a ledger and started keeping track of all sales, wholesale and retail, and started keeping all receipts for anything connected to the business. Yes, when you self-publish a book, you are in business and must do all the things necessary to keep it afloat.

My limited computer skills got me through the Amazon requirements for setting up my author account. I used the same basic biography that I used in my books. Key words, such as West Texas, Crime, Texas Ranger, Sheriff, were added to guide readers to my book. Amazon (and later Kindle) sales are directly deposited in a bank account that I set up specifically for the book business. (All retail and wholesale book sale monies are also deposited there.)

THE MOVIES

There is no doubt that I believe **The Gun That Wasn't There** would make a great movie. That is why so many books were mailed to those in that business; only most of them were returned unopened and unread. A few from magazines, such as The Oprah Magazine, were also returned with something like, "Unfortunately, we are unable to accept your piece for review."

Letters from Warner Brothers and 20th Century Fox indicated that they only accept material from literary agents connected to the Screen Writers Guild. Finally, I learned about a bullet list whereby the author's vision of the movie could be cast onto one piece of paper. I produced one for **The Gun That Wasn't There** - but again received a number of letters similar to what I had already received.

I have continued to send copies to popular movie stars and anyone who I believe could get the book before the right people. I've done this because I believe the story has merit and because of the saying, "Dream as if you will live forever... Live as if you only have today," - Anonymous.

Of course, over the years two things connected to the movies did increase my heart rate.

The first occurred after I sent the bullet list page to Castle Rock Entertainment, Inc. On March 6, 2009, I received a phone call from a woman who said she worked for the company. It was the right area code and the right name in the phone identification system. She asked me to confirm my contact information, that her boss who was head of acquisitions had asked her to do so. I have been waiting but I've never heard from them since.

The other thing involves something that I will cherish forever. Clint Eastwood was on the list of people who received one of the first 50 books. It was sent to his Carmel, California Post Office Box. Many months later I received a package from Malposo Productions in Burbank, California. It contained an autographed portrait of Clint Eastwood from the movie Million Dollar Baby. I had it matted and framed and it now hangs in my office.

I have contacted a number of agents over the years but none have taken interest in this project. My next step would probably be to join the Screen Writers Guild and write my own complete vision in script format. However, I have a lot of things on my plate and haven't gotten around to it.

The Gun That Wasn't There
By Russell S. Smith

- Midnight. Caveman Bandit jumps from moving boxcar in West Texas. He breaks into occupied home. Someone awakes; he places hand on his pistol. Snores resume. He leaves taking food and woman's nightgown.
- Burglaries begin in Val Verde and Terrell Counties.
- June 1965. Sanderson flood claims 26 lives. Burglaries continue.
- July 1965. Midnight. Bandit shoots Postmaster at Pumpville, kidnaps Postmaster's wife; makes her open safe. Steals their money and car.
- Burglaries continue.
- November 1965. Near cave in Thurston Canyon. Bandit shoots Terrell County Sheriff. Rushed to hospital, Sheriff survives with permanent sciatic nerve damage and loss of spleen.
- Nine month manhunt begins –
  Dog Cactus stops bloodhounds.
  Posse heads toward Tex/Mex border; Bandit circles back to Dryden.
- Burglaries continue
- 1966. Early morning. Dark. Texas Rangers hear Bandit approaching; then quiet.
- Deputy and Highway Patrolman turn over car/trailer w/horses rushing to sighting.
- Woman meets Bandit behind her house at Dryden, sends him away.
- Woman's daughter chases sheep from railroad tracks. Sheep runs into brush; Bandit runs out other side.
- Hidden camps are found in dense brush. Cooking camps, sleeping camps.
- Bandit verbally threatens rancher.
- August 1966. Midnight. Bandit returns to Pumpville. Rancher fires shot in air.
- August 19, 1966. Midnight. Texas Ranger and hobbling Sheriff stake out station/café/store in Dryden. Bandit comes first night; burglarizes store. Ranger, Sheriff and Bandit have their own shootout at O.K. Corral; 17 shots fired, Bandit repeatedly falls and gets up, still shooting. Ranger's last shot finally brings culprit to justice.
- Bandit sentenced to prison. Threatens to come back and kill everyone involved.
- Paroled 1984, possibly seen near Dryden 1986. Never seen again – or was he?

For a review copy of this true crime account, please contact author Russell S. Smith, P.O. Box 62702, San Angelo, Texas 76902. (325) 234-7407 cell (325) 949-7182 email: fiftysixsouth@yahoo.com website: www.russellssmith.com

One Page Bullet List

LISTEN TO THOSE IN THE BUSINESS

I have tried to listen to those in the book business and to my customers during my book venture. It was Felton Cochran and Elmer Kelton who told me if the woman (Jean Hardy) who owned Front Street Books in Alpine liked **The Gun That Wasn't There**, that the book would have promise. I stopped by her business on my initial trip and left a copy for her to review. She has handled the book since and I greatly appreciate her advice and suggestions.

MARKETING

I am sure that most self-published authors dream of having a big time publisher pick up their book and take it out into the national market. It does happen on occasion but most times it is the author, with a good story, who makes his or her book business a success. An appropriate saying is, "The desire to succeed is useless without the willingness to prepare." – Anonymous.

After seven years, I can tell you that marketing a book (or books) is really just work. Many of my sales directly correlate to something I have done myself, or the post product of stories written by others or by word of mouth. However you look at it though, the self-published author is only getting started when he sees the first book in his hand.

Advertising Materials

Posters promoting the book or books were produced for use in the retail markets. If I made one mistake, it was that I made too many such materials. At times, I've made others, giving readers something new to see that might catch their eye. Quotes from readers make good copy, especially words like those from Don W. Jackson from Sheffield, Texas shortly after he read **The Gun That Wasn't There**. "Russell. You have hit a home run with your book. No one has ever captured the people and the country west of the Pecos as you have. It is possibly the best true crime story I have read. It should be made into a movie."

Adobe Photoshop software was used to produce posters advertising Russell Smith's books.

Business cards have been one of the most cost productive things that I have used. I have put them inside each book sold, have them on the table at book-signings and events, and carry them everywhere I go. As an example, I've given away nearly a hundred while on vacation. This increases Amazon sales – because I don't give them to anyone except those I strike up a conversation with. At times, I've felt that I make one sale for every five I give out.

Business cards have been one of the most cost productive things Russell Smith has ever used to promote his books.

One Christmas season I mailed postcards advertising **The Gun That Wasn't There** to many businesses within my readership area. My idea was to suggest they buy the book as gifts for their clients, family and/or friends. One company did order enough to pay for my costs but that was all. Today, I look on that venture as an education that broke even.

Christmas cards are much less costly than commercially produced post cards.

Commercial Ads

I just knew that people would flock to Amazon and buy cases of **The Gun That Wasn't There** if they saw an ad in a national publication like American Handgunner or American Cowboy. Even the line ads were expensive but I just knew they were the ticket to success. Yet, for me, the only ads that really worked were local and regional ads. This brings to mind something that Felton Cochran and Ross McSwain told me several times, "Your books are regional."

Book-signings

Many authors are asked to do booksignings in businesses where their books are sold. The authors sign their books and the business gets the sale. These locations have been a real blessing for me, getting to meet and greet people and getting a real education in the process.

I have repeatedly watched as people start scanning books on a shelf. When a book's cover grabs their attention, they turn, and may or may not pick it up. If they do, most turn it over and read the tidbits on the back. Some put it back down, maybe realizing it is not the genre they like to read, while others either turn to the front and start reading the first few pages, or they put it in their basket. If it is nonfiction, they may scan through any pictures before making a decision.

"Get them to sign their name on a pad before signing it to them," Elmer Kelton told me when I published my first book. I should have listened to him better because one of the mistakes I've made is to sign books incorrectly, thereby ruining the copy. Now I try to take the time to gather my thoughts about the inscription – and I always ask them to spell the name if I have any doubt. (I have found that (for me) Gel-type pens move more freely across the page.)

I have also made the mistake of signing the wrong book. **<u>No Reason to Kill</u>** and **<u>Steps into God's Country</u>** have basically the same spine width. A woman picked up a copy that was turned toward me. I "thought" it was the book about the 1980 jewelry store death of 20-year-old Sheila Elrod. I had several copies laying in front of me so I personalized one to her and handed it to her. Only she wanted a copy of the book that guides readers through my outdoor memoirs and heritage – **<u>Steps into God's Country</u>**.

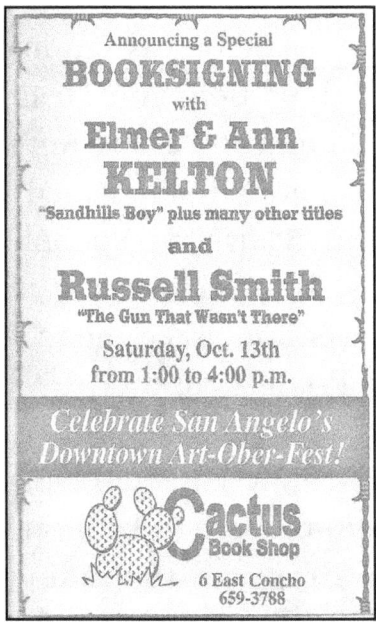

Businesses that sell books sometimes advertise their book-signing events.

I normally produce a press release about each of my booksignings and send it to the local media organizations. Any notice in the press can let readers know where you will be and when.

Public Speaking

I was pretty shy as a kid and still shy when I entered police work. Yet a transfer into the Crime Prevention – Crime Stoppers section led me to attend different luncheons and events as I represented the San Angelo Police Dept.

My first Thursday in the assignment took me to a noon meeting of the Safety and Health Committee of the Chamber of Commerce. There were about 30 people I didn't know who were already seated when I arrived. I sat down to visit with a few media people who were sitting at a table nearby. Bob Diebitsch, the Chamber Vice-President, came over and asked me to sit with the larger group. I told him I'd be right over.

When he walked away, I asked the media folks, "By the way, what are we doing here today?" Suddenly, you could have heard a pin drop and the radio person sitting to my right whispered, "Don't you know? You are the guest speaker."

I have been speaking publicly ever since, and it has come in handy when promoting my books. Most of my talks have been given to civic clubs, especially those that allow me to peddle my books after the meeting. Most presentations are 20 minutes long with a little additional time for questions. For several years I used large foamboard backed photographs to promote my historical works, but today I have progressed to a PowerPoint projector and screen.

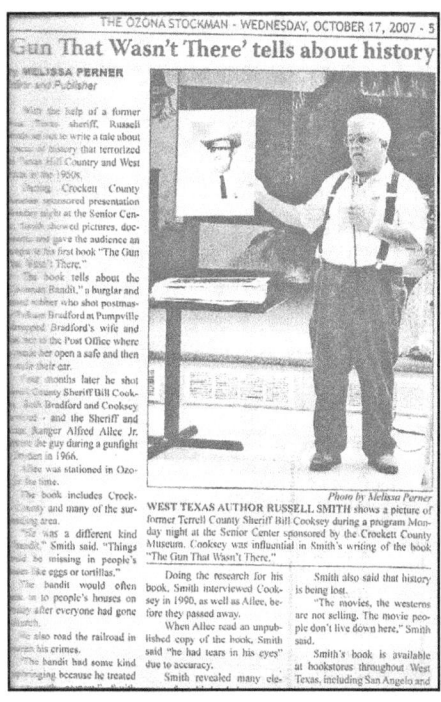

Russell Smith used to use large foam-board backed photographs to promote his books but today uses a PowerPoint projector and screen.

The Nickel Tour

I believe that every author needs a nickel tour to properly promote his or her work. These are a few sentences that describe the book as it garners interest.

My nickel tour example might be: **<u>The Gun That Wasn't There</u>** is the story of a Bandit who terrorized parts of the Texas Hill Country and West Texas during the 1960s. In July 1965, he shot the Postmaster at Pumpville, in Val Verde County, and four months later shot the Sheriff of Terrell County. A 9-month manhunt begins that ends with a shootout that involves the hobbling Sheriff and a Texas Ranger.

A question I nearly always get afterwards is, "What does **<u>The Gun That Wasn't There</u>** have to do with it?" I always say, "You'll have to buy the book to find out." (The title can be the key to getting a person's attention.)

Booth Sales

Booth sales have been a mixed bag for me. I have purchased booth space at a number of different events during the last seven years. Book fairs, historical meetings, community weekend events and gun shows are not as costly as the San Angelo Stock Show and Rodeo and Christmas at Old Fort Concho that I've done for the last several years. (These later events do draw thousands of people into their craft-product sales area.)

Setting up a booth has involved the fee to be there, the costs of portable tables and chairs that can be carried here and there. Sturdy cloth was purchased so my wife could sew three tablecloths that wrap around the front and sides of our tables.

I made one mistake early on at my first Stock Show. I set up a monitor and ran a looping PowerPoint presentation about **The Gun That Wasn't There**. A few of my books were on set-up stands nearby. The book was fairly new but sales were not going like I wanted. I hadn't even recovered the booth fee much less food and the cost of the books. A few days before the event was over, a woman named Linda Hogue, who sold toys, asked if I'd mind a little suggestion.

"Do you have a lot of copies of your book?" she asked. Soon the PowerPoint equipment had been removed and books were stacked chest-high all over the table. We sold 197 copies before the week's end.

Aside from the expense of buying the booth space, event contracts may require your booth to be open and manned during every hour the event is open to the public. This becomes a manpower issue with events such as the rodeo that has twelve-hour days over a span of two weeks.

*Russell Smith's booth at the San
Angelo Stock Show and Rodeo.*

Awards and Contests

Winning a writing award or contest adds to your resume and may get others to notice you. I don't normally enter such things though my book **Steps into God's Country** was recognized with a Texas Outdoor Writers Assn. Excellence-in-Craft first place award in 2013. A notice and a poster were sent to the retail outlets – helping readers realize the depth of the work.

Texas Country Reporter

Brian Hawkins, a producer and videographer for the Texas Country Reporter television show, called me on a Monday night in Oct. 2010. He spent the following

Thursday and Friday in San Angelo, talking to me on camera about **The Gun That Wasn't There**. The story ran several months later and the response on Amazon and through Kindle sales was amazing.

The Amazon bestseller rank for the book went crazy for a few days – sending the book to 20,380 in overall books and #7 in the History-Americas-Mexico category. My Kindle sales soared to #9 in the Kindle Nonfiction Criminal Law category. These higher rankings lasted for about ten days.

Location, Location, Location

There is no doubt that where your books are located can make a difference in how many are sold. Books placed at eye-level, at the end of a row or in special containers designed to grab the customers attention can really help. However, it is the store owner or managers who make those decisions. My books have been in both good placement locations and also on the bottom shelf. It is what it is and out of my hands.

A business located along an Interstate sold more of my books in six months than any other place. This was because of impulse buying – a term attached to the person paying a bill for something who grabs another product beside the cash register. This is why magazines are in the racks next to the check out at grocery stores and why candy and knickknacks are always there. The sales slowed dramatically when more items were added and the products moved to a table away from the payout area.

In my booths, I try to have some of the books at eye-level so the masses can see them even though they are walking on the other side of the aisle. Again, the whole table is stacked with books as previously mentioned.

Lynn's Advice

Lynn, the CreateSpace publishing consultant, told me right off that I should put the books on Kindle and set up a website with a blog, use Facebook, Twitter and other social media to help drive sales. I did set up a static website (www.russellssmith.com) and I use Facebook occasionally. However, needless to say, I wish I had put the books on Kindle sooner, but it was years before I did it.

"I'm not going to buy another one of your books until you put them on Kindle," said a woman who works at the bank. Those words encouraged me to pay the fee to put the first three books on Kindle. Sales started immediately. Authors are paid a royalty for all books sold through Kindle and Amazon – the author does not have any cost in that product (except the Kindle initial setup fee).

THE 2% CLUB

The Gun That Wasn't There was a popular book from the beginning. It was not long before my first 1000 books were nearly gone. I knew it was time to re-order. Lynn was off that day so I talked to someone else. "I would like to order another 1000 books," I told her.

"So you're a member of the 2% Club," said the consultant. She explained, after I asked, that only 2% of people who self-publish ever re-order. "Most probably have them sitting in their garage," said the woman.

Of course, this was in 2007. I don't know what the stats are now, only what she told me then. However, it is something that has stuck with me over the years.

MORE ABOUT MY BUSINESS

My relationship with Amazon and CreateSpace has evolved into an efficient system for me. Via email, I get weekly sales updates from CreateSpace and monthly updates on sales and monies from Amazon and CreateSpace. I can log into the CreateSpace website at any time and go to my "Member Dashboard" and see sales, order more books, contact support or start another book.

Research Materials

Writing nonfiction involves gathering and paying for documents, photographs, video tapes and assorted digital information that take up space in my small office by the time the book is completed. I need that space to research my next book so the materials from my first few books have been given to Angelo State University's West Texas Collection.

Scrapbooks

Scrapbooks (3-ring binders) have been produced for each book. There are five now for **<u>The Gun That Wasn't</u>**

There. Inside are letters and cards from readers or those who were connected to that part of history; newspaper and magazine stories highlighting the book; booksigning announcements; photographs from presentations dealing with the book and any correction or addition to that part of history. These books will someday make their way to the West Texas Collection.

Write on 5th Grade Level

An instructor in one writing class said you should write on a 5th grade level if you want everyone to read what you write. I would add that you should write to your audience.

Other Mistakes

Care for your product. Spilled Gatorade ruined three copies of my inventory after I put the box in the floorboard below one of my grandkids.

Listen to those who sell books. I have been fortunate to have great mentors as I researched, wrote and now sell books. Yet, I cannot stress enough, that much of my effort was only after talks with Cactus Book Shop owner Felton Cochran and others in the book business. If you are going to sell <u>physical</u> books – the people who sell them are great resources.

Hurry and you may lose. The research materials for **<u>No Reason to Kill</u>** involved 96 three-ring binders full of documents and materials, video tapes, cassettes and hundreds of photographs. Putting the book together so it was easy to read and understand was quite a task. Yet I hurried, at the end, because Christmas was coming. I hurried and mistakenly left out several pages about Kerrville. I lost an account in the process.

Encrypt your eBook files. This was not my mistake but one that kept me from putting my books on Kindle for a while. I was at a book fair. A professional photographer had the booth across from me. He was very upset. He'd just learned that someone had stolen his book files, had copies printed, and was selling them in retail outlets along the West Coast.

MY FINAL THOUGHTS ABOUT BOOKS

Our ever changing world has touched the book business just like everything else. While I like to physically hold a book and see the words on a page, you see the Kindle, tablets or other information devices everywhere today. It is why I originally decided to go with a company connected to Amazon.

How many people actually read books? A Jenkins Group, Inc. survey I found on Wiki.answers.com reported – 1/3 of high school grads never read another book; 42% of college grads never read another book; 70% of adults haven't been in a bookstore in the last five years; and 70% of books published do not make a profit.

My personal observations, after years of watching people walk by my booth at different events, has led me to believe that only 15% of people actually read books and those are divided about half and half as to who reads nonfiction versus fiction. People who pick up a book will buy it about 20% of the time. Give them your nickel tour and that increases to about 40%. Many would not stop at all were it not for the cover design.

Writing books was a dream I didn't accomplish until my 50s. However, the business of peddling books is something else altogether. It is a lot of work. If you have long dreamed of writing your own book, I'd suggest you do that – write it (in your own words). Then you can worry about editing, how to get it published and the work that follows later.

ABOUT THE AUTHOR

Russell S. Smith was born in Uvalde, Texas. He started writing poems and short stories long before he graduated from high school in 1969. He attended Southwest Texas Junior College, Howard College and Angelo State University; the majority of his classes dealt with criminal justice.

His law enforcement career began as a reserve deputy with the Tom Green County Sheriff's Department in 1977 and ended when he retired as San Angelo's Police Chief in 1999. This experience spurred his professional writing career when he sold his first article to a police trade magazine in 1980. Russell was appointed as a Tom Green County Justice of the Peace in 2003. Unopposed in the following elections, he retired December 31, 2010.

From 1998 to 2003, Russell was an outdoor columnist for the San Angelo Standard-Times and several magazines. **The Gun That Wasn't There** was his first non-fiction book. His second was **No Reason to Kill;** about the murder of Sheila Elrod, a 20-year-old San Angelo woman killed during a jewelry store robbery in 1980. His third was **<u>One Policeman's Lights and Siren</u>** which is a collection of short stories about his early police career. His outdoor memoirs "**<u>Steps into God's Country</u>**" comes after writing in the outdoor field for nearly 30 years.

Russell has received numerous awards over the years for his writing and photography from the Texas Outdoor Writers' Association. He now writes a periodic outdoor column for the San Angelo Standard-Times as he researches other projects and writes from his home in San Angelo, Texas. He and his wife Linda have been married 40 years. They have two married children and four grandchildren.

www.ingramcontent.com/pod-product-compliance
Lightning Source LLC
Chambersburg PA
CBHW070555290526
45790CB00002B/696